THE PLURALISM

workbook

Identifiers: ISBN 979-8-9921157-0-3 (paperback)

Published by Spectrum Editions

In memory of Samantha Woll
one of the world's great connectors

We live in a world that is increasingly polarized and divided. Talking with people who are different from us is quickly becoming a lost art. This workbook guides you step-by-step through techniques that will allow you to listen better, share your point of view more effectively, and keep talking with each other when the conversation gets challenging.

Why Do I Want
TO DO THIS?

write here

PART I: PERSONAL GROWTH

How will talking to people outside my community benefit me as a person? Will it help me professionally? Will it spur personal growth?

Why Do I Want
TO DO THIS?

write here

PART II: WORLD BUILDING

How will the world be better if I learn to engage
with people who think differently from me?

Why Do I Want

TO DO THIS?

write here

PART III: EVERYTHING ELSE

Think of three other ways learning to engage with
people who think differently
will be helpful to you and others!

Hard is good

_____

_____

_____

_____

_____

_____

_____

Seven hard things I love

How could talking with people who disagree be hard?

1. I could get 'cancelled'
2. I might feel embarrassed
3.

HOW WILL I CONQUER MY FEARS?

Write the two scariest possibilities from the last page below. Then make a game plan on the next page for how you will tackle them.

_____

_____

MY BRAVERY GAME PLANS

IMAGINE

YOUR
PARTNER
in dialogue

These are things I imagine
about people
who think differently
from me

(It's okay, you can tear this page out later...)

AND... HERE'S WHAT I *Suspect* THEY THINK

ABOUT ME...

_____

_____

_____

_____

——— ❖ ———

——— ❖ ———

——— ❖ ———

——— ❖ ———

a list

——— ❖ ———

——— ❖ ———

——— ❖ ———

——— ❖ ———

Of things we probably have in common

Bad things
my friends or family say
will happen
if I talk with people
who think differently:

Good things that could happen instead:

What are the <u>costs</u>

OF NOT TALKING

to people who are different?

brainstorm here

It's not just about ideas.
When I think about talking to
folks who are different,
I worry that I'll <u>feel</u>:

1. Awkward and silly.
2. Attacked for my identity.
3.
4.
5.
6.
7.
8.
9.
10.

I can calm myself by:

1. **DOODLING**
2. **DEEP BREATHS**
3.
4.
5.
6.
7.
8.
9.
10.
11.
12.

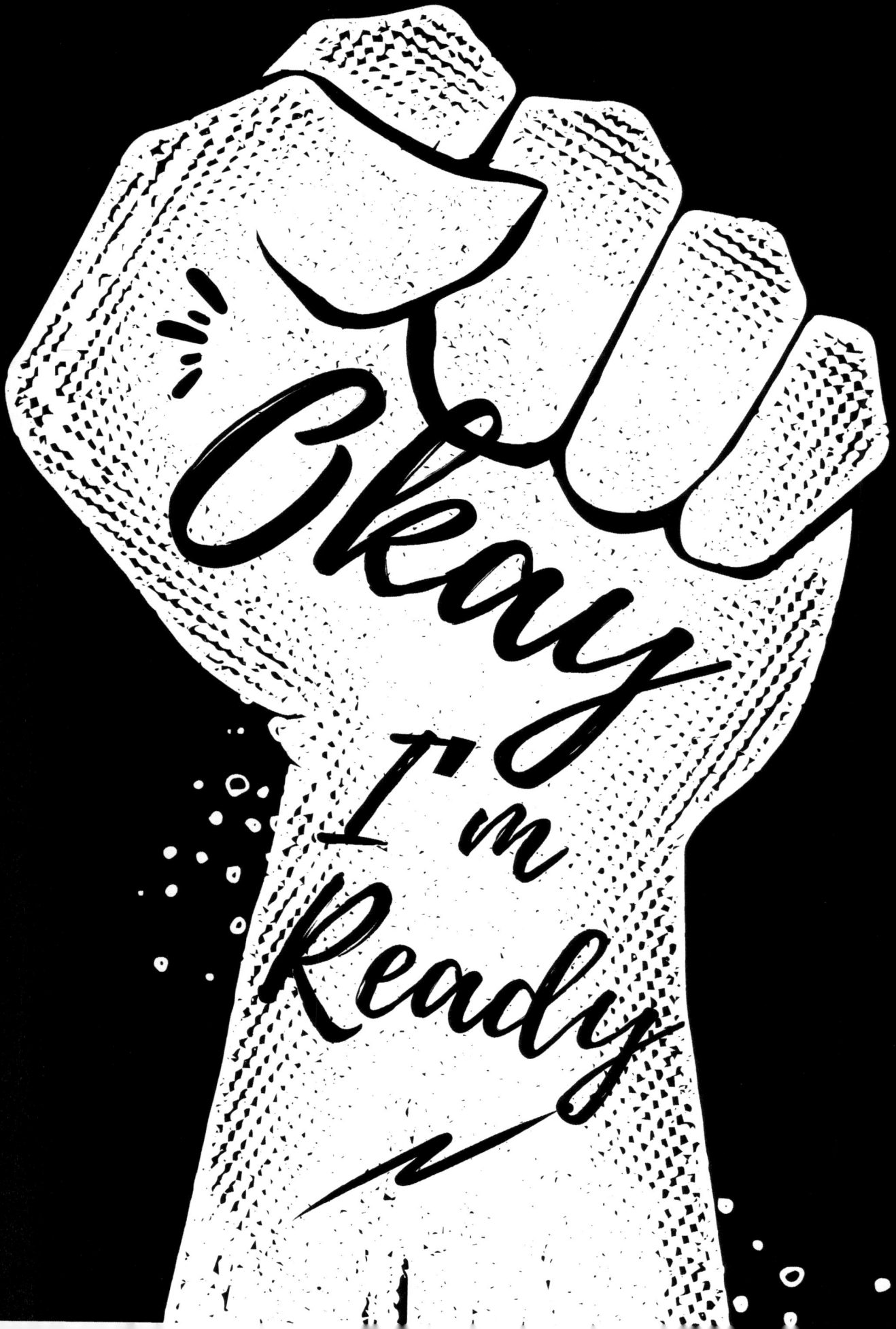

Where I'll find

PEOPLE WHO DIFFER

AT WORK
_____

IN CLASS
_____

_____

_____

_____

BUILD A
FOUNDATION FIRST

How will I establish common ground?

Finding interests in
common can go a long
way toward steadying
the relationship when
you disagree.

What interests do I have that
could help me connect? Pets?
Family? Hobbies? Write them
in the boxes!

01

02

03

04

05

06

PEOPLE FEEL SAFE WHEN THEY FEEL SEEN

WHAT ARE SOME THINGS THAT YOU WANT PEOPLE TO SEE AND APPRECIATE ABOUT <u>YOU</u>?

PEOPLE FEEL SAFE WHEN THEY FEEL SEEN

WHAT ARE SOME QUALITIES YOU MIGHT SEE AND APPRECIATE IN <u>SOMEONE ELSE</u>?

Integrity

Making an effort to be kind

CONVERSATIONAL TURBO

chargers

Bring out the best in someone
by moving beyond small talk.
Ask them something surprising
like "What are you excited
about these days?"

Think up some creative questions:

1.

2.

3.

4.

5.

6.

7.

Communities are held together by little things. The sound of your own name. A smile.

WHAT LITTLE THINGS WILL
YOU DO TO MAKE PEOPLE
FEEL SECURE?

_____

_____

_____

_____

_____

_____

HOW WILL YOU GET YOURSELF
CALM | CONFIDENT | COMFORTABLE?

I'LL BRING TEA

I'LL SMILE TO PUT MYSELF IN A GOOD MOOD

Body  language

HOW WILL I KEEP MY BODY
CALM AND OPEN?

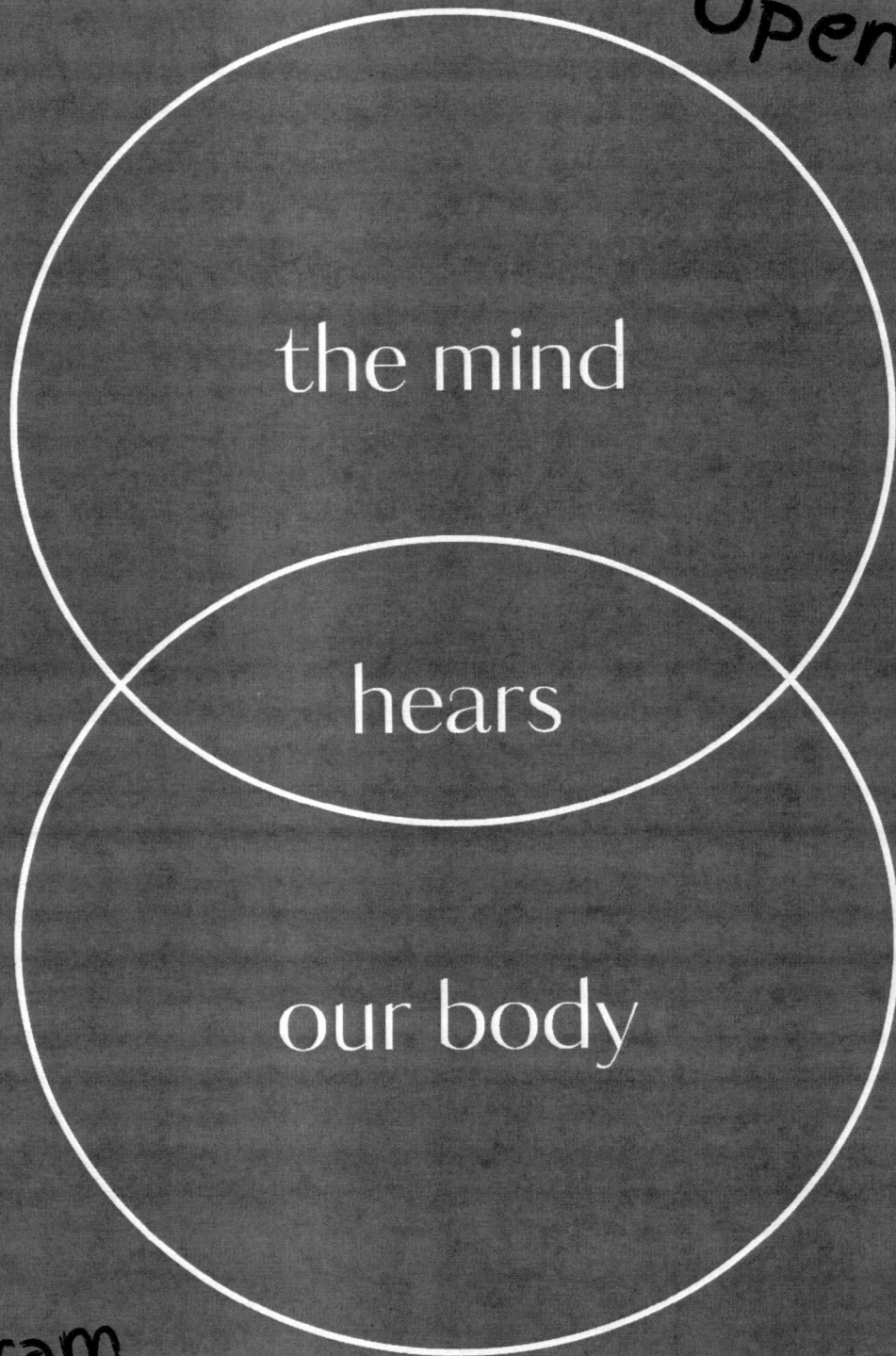

Open hands

the mind

hears

our body

Diaphram
Breathing

_____

_____

_____

_____

_____

_____

_____

_____

_____

_____

_____

How will I make sure my body language conveys interest and attention?

How I can listen more actively?

1. Instead of thinking about what I will say next, I'll identify open-ended questions that will enhance my understanding.

2. I'll ask more questions than feels natural.

3.

4.

5.

6.

7.

8.

9.

10.

Subtext Matters
HOW CAN I LISTEN BEYOND THE WORDS?

01

What is the Emotion? -

What emotion informs the speaker? Are they confused? Sad? Anxious?

02

Why Does the Speaker Think This?

Did they hear this from their grandmother? Read a book? Learn it at church?

03

04

05

06

BE GENUINELY CURIOUS ABOUT OTHERS

VALIDATE OTHERS' FEELINGS.

IMAGINE YOURSELF IN OTHERS' SHOES.

LISTEN WITH EMPATHY

WHAT DOES THAT MEAN TO YOU?

WRITE MORE HERE

YOU CAN VALIDATE + WITHOUT AGREEING

YOU CAN VALIDATE OTHERS BY SHOWING THAT YOU'RE LISTENING

hmmm is a good listening sound

if i don't want to nod. I can...

WHAT WILL YOU DO TO SHOW YOU'RE LISTENING?

YOU CAN VALIDATE OTHERS BY ACKNOWLEDGING THEIR FEELINGS

it sounds like you feel strongly about this

WHAT COULD YOU SAY TO ACKNOWLEDGE THE SPEAKER'S FEELINGS?

How Can I Be Curious?

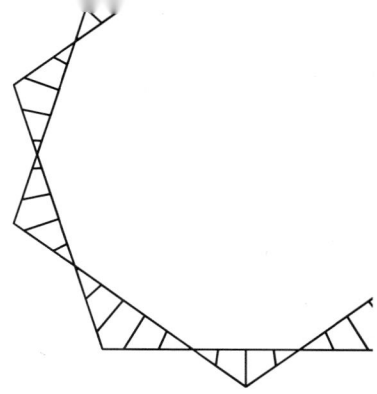

LISTENING WITH CURIOSITY

WHY DO THEY...
THINK THIS?
USE THAT WORD?

WHAT DO THEY...
VALUE?
RESPECT?
FEAR?

HOW DO THEY...
USE EVIDENCE?
CHANGE THEIR MIND?

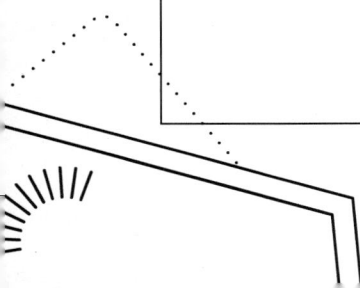

THEIR SHOES

LISTEN TO SEE
HOW THEIR LIFE IS
DIFFERENT FROM YOURS

Home

Social Issues

Health

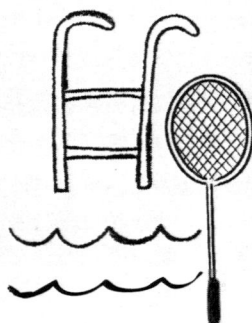

WE CAN'T KNOW EVERYTHING THAT SOMEONE IS FACING.

Finances

What might you
learn about each
of these areas?

NO NEED TO BE
NOSY!

HOW CAN YOU
LEARN THINGS
JUST FROM
LISTENING?

CHECK
—YOUR FEELINGS—

HOW HAVE THESE WORDS AFFECTED ME?

YOU CAN ONLY FULLY
UNDERSTAND
A CONVERSATION
IF YOU UNDERSTAND
HOW IT MAKES YOU
FEEL

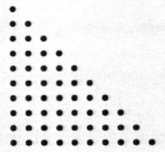

I KNOW I'M FEELING THINGS

when

MY BODY

My hands feel sweaty, my throat feels tight...

MY THOUGHTS

My brain starts to race, I miss parts of the conversation...

THE ROOM

Feels too hot...

But Sometimes

YOUR FIRST FEELING ISN'T ALWAYS THE REAL FEELING...

I FELT___*angry*___

When....

BUT DEEP DOWN I WAS:

embarrassed because...

I FELT_____

When.....

BUT DEEP DOWN I WAS:

_____ because...

I FELT_____

When.....

BUT DEEP DOWN I WAS:

_____ because...

THE FIND YOUR
REAL FEELING
EXERCISE

HOW BETTER LISTENING

Benefits Me

1. CONFLICT BECOMES MORE COMFORTABLE.

2. PEOPLE LISTEN BACK.

3. I BECOME MORE EMPATHETIC.

4.

5.

6.

7.

8.

9.

10.

11.

12.

THINK OF A CONVERSATION THAT WENT WRONG

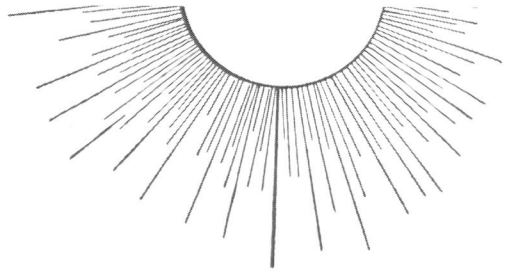

How could the listening techniques you just outlined have changed the outcome of that conversation?

NOW

It's time
to
talk

Let your emotions settle before you respond

PAUSE AND CALM BEFORE REPLYING

PHRASES I CAN SAY
to buy myself a moment

I just need a minute to digest before I respond...

That's a lot to take in. Give me one second before I reply?

affect how **you** **perceive** the conversation

I expected him to be a jerk...and he was! I think...?

I thought she was an ally...but maybe she wasn't really so on our side in the end?

Think of a conversation you had recently

_____

_____

How did you expect the conversation to go?

How did it go?

ASK YOURSELF:
WHAT JUDGMENTS, ASSUMPTIONS, AND EMOTIONS

DO I BRING TO THE TOPIC?

UNPACK YOUR REACTIONS
TO A CHALLENGING ISSUE HERE TO PRACTICE

sometimes a topic will press your buttons

- Talking about gender ⟶ Can make me feel defensive

- The word 'listen...' ⟶ Makes me feel disrespected

it can help to notice when that happens

SOMETHING ELSE

i think she talks about gender	because she wants me to understand her experience

he says 'listen' a lot...	maybe it's just something he says when he's nervous?

TRY TO IMAGINE WHAT

IF...

they show me
my assumptions
WERE WRONG...

...how will I
deal with
that?

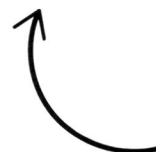

GAME PLAN HERE

HOW DO I GET OVER

the embarrassment if I assumed something that wasn't true (about a person or topic)?

01 - I could tell myself:

Mistakes lead to learning

02- I could focus on their feelings by:

03- I could ask questions such as:

04 - I could restate the new idea by:

WHAT COULD I SAY TO SIGNAL THAT I WAS WRONG?

_____

_____

_____

_____

_____

_____

_____

_____

YOU MIGHT BEGIN WITH THE TRIPLE "A" TECHNIQUE:

ACKNOWLEDGE

AFFIRM

ASK

Things I can Say

I think I heard you say....?

I see what you mean...

_____

_____

_____

_____

_____

_____

TO ACKNOWLEDGE WHAT
SOMEONE SAID

Things I can Say

Thanks for being so open.
I appreciate your honesty

_____

_____

_____

_____

_____

_____

TO AFFIRM THE SPEAKER,
EVEN IF DON'T AGREE

BUT IF YOU DO AGREE

You should

say so...

Admit it when someone
makes a good point

WHEN THEY KNOW
YOU'RE LISTENING
THEY WILL LISTEN BACK

WHAT CLARIFYING QUESTIONS COULD YOU ASK

What did you mean by...?

Could you give an example of....?

TO UNDERSTAND THE OTHER PERSON'S POINT BETTER?

How do you feel about that?

digging deeper:

What open-ended questions could you ask to understand the other person's position better?

What do you really *want to say?*

I prioritize points I think might convince the listener...

I prioritize the point I personally care most about...

We can only absorb a little new information at one time. How do you decide which point(s) you want to make?

People listen better

when you surprise them

write here ⟶

Can you think of arguments or examples that deviate
from the usual talking points?
Try it now with three issues that you care about.

BEFORE YOU SHARE
plan your tone

- [ ] Will I sound defensive?
- [ ] Will I sound like I care?
- [ ] ....
- [ ] ....
- [ ] ....
- [ ] ....
- [ ] ....
- [ ] ....
- [ ] ....
- [ ] ....
- [ ] ....

OPEN WITH
Vulnerability

I'm a little nervous talking about this because....

This issue is really important to me because...

WHAT ARE SOME THINGS YOU CAN SAY TO SHARE WHERE YOU ARE COMING FROM?

Then state your

Intention

Brainstorm some intention formulas here

Why do you want other people to hear what you're about to say? Are you looking for them to understand your situation? Do you want to persuade them of something?

it can also help

to highlight
where you agree

What are some ways you can show others
how you're on the same side?

We both want....
_____

I also care a lot about....
_____

_____

_____

_____

_____

_____

_____

_____

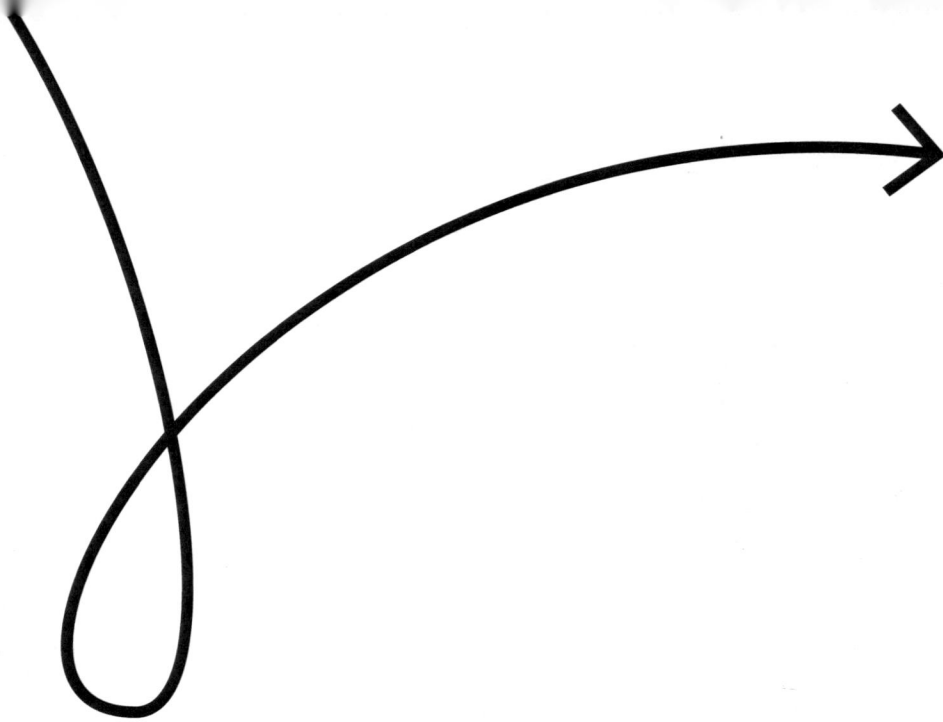

People listen more
receptively when y<u>ou</u>
talk in a way that is

open

flexible

respectful

curious

exploratory

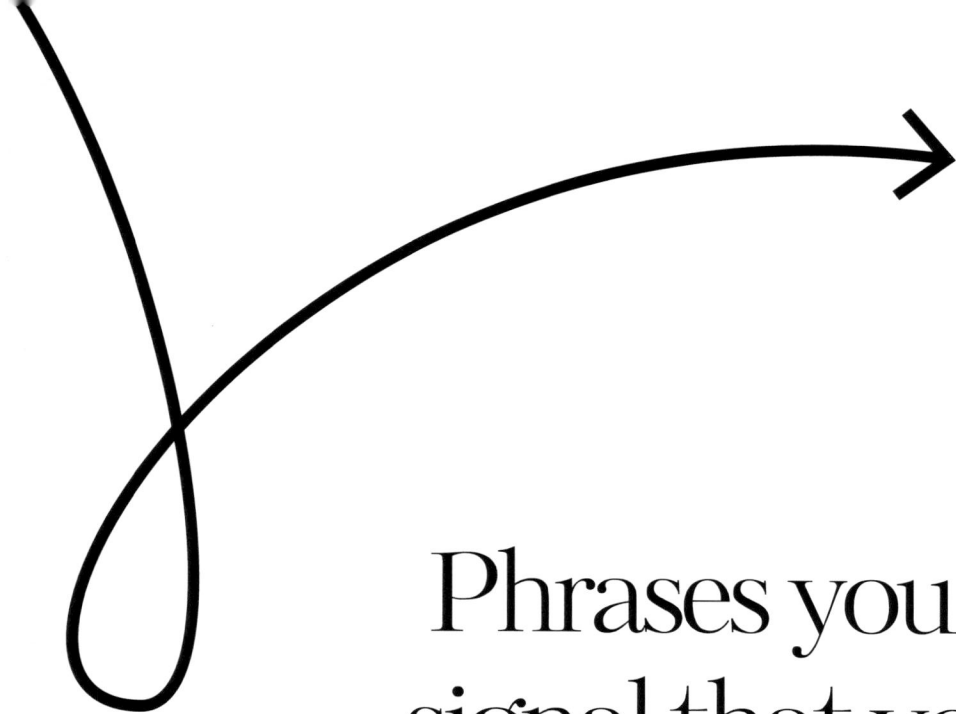

Phrases you can use to signal that you are open to other positions:

Personally, I think...

In my own experience...

Phrases you can use to signal that you are willing to change your mind:

I'm open to changing my mind but....

_____

I'm willing to be convinced otherwise but...

_____

_____

_____

_____

Phrases you can use to signal a respectful difference of opinion:

I hear you, but I see things another way...

I'm not entirely convinced, it seems to me...

Phrases you can use to show curiosity and a willingness to explore:

Could it be that.....?

Would it change your mind if...?

How can you tailor your message to your audience?

I can use words I think they will know...
_____

I'll stick to experiences we share when I give examples...
_____

_____

_____

_____

_____

Try to imagine how your audience

will hear things

words that might brush someone the wrong way	words I could use instead
Fundamentalist →	*Religious*
→	
→	
→	
→	
→	

and adjust your language accordingly

THE POWER
of Yes

I think we can both agree that….

PRACTICE THE ART OF BUY IN PHRASES | OPEN WITH IDEAS
THEY CAN SAY YES TO BEFORE
YOU MOVE ON TO IDEAS
WITH WHICH THEY DISAGREE

Then identify

Where we don't agree yet is....

Imagine a core disagreement on a topic you you care about here to practice!

THE CORE ISSUE

On which you disagree → So you can address it without distraction

Don't let your conversation get bogged down in side issues.

HOW CAN I SHOW

THEY MISSED SOMETHING

WITHOUT CONTRADICTING?

brainstorm useful phrases here

How will I explain if a 'fact' isn't true?

I also heard that stastistic on Youtube! But I read an article recently that proved that number was actually made up!

politely....

HOW CAN I INTRODUCE
NEW EVIDENCE

IN A WAY
THAT IS EASY
TO HEAR?

I've been doing some research and...

In my personal experience...

I was personally surprised to hear this, but did you realize...

Practice being Concise

Pick a piece of evidence and write it out here

_____
_____
_____
_____
_____
_____

Identify the key components

Now write it shorter

_____
_____
_____
_____
_____
_____
_____

And shorter...

_____
_____
_____
_____
_____
_____
_____

TO PERSUADE
SOMEONE

YOU HAVE
TO ADDRESS

THEIR

OBJECTIONS

WHAT DOUBTS
DO YOU NEED TO DISPEL?

Here are five ways

I can figure out

why someone disagrees:

I can notice what statements make them squirmy...

_____

_____

_____

_____

_____

BRAINSTORM WAYS TO ADDRESS DIFFERENT KINDS OF OBJECTIONS

If an idea feels uncomfortable to them because it's new, I can talk about how I got used to the idea myself

Can you

TELL A STORY?

STORIES BRING PEOPLE INTO YOUR EXPERIENCE

What are some stories that have influenced *your* positions?

_____

_____

_____

_____

_____

YOU COULD TELL A STORY ABOUT AN EXPERIENCE THAT SHAPED YOUR OPINION

PRACTICE THAT HERE

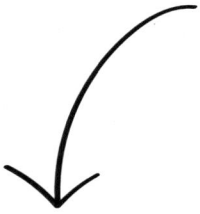

TRY TO USE VIVID IMAGERY,
DETAILS, AND FEELINGS
LANGUAGE

YOU COULD TELL A STORY ABOUT WHY YOU CHANGED YOUR OWN POSITION

PRACTICE THAT HERE

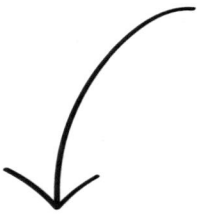

TRY TO CAPTURE HOW YOU USED TO FEEL AND WHAT IT WAS LIKE TO CHANGE YOUR MIND

listeners respond to

EVIDENCE

statistics

personal experiences

when you give proof for your ideas. You show respect

What kinds of evidence do you personally find convincing?

evidence

is most convincing

when it is offered in groups of three. saying too much can seem manipulative. saying too little can seem disrespectful.

brainstorm

1. _____

2. _____

3. _____

PRACTICE CHOOSING YOUR BEST POINTS

FIRST WRITE *ALL* YOUR EVIDENCE FOR AN IDEA. THEN PICK YOUR THREE *BEST* PROOFS.

fun fact

positive evidence

PERSUADES

better than

negative evidence

TURN THAT SMILE UPSIDE DOWN

PRACTICE **RESTATING**

NEGATIVE EVIDENCE AS **POSITIVE EVIDENCE**

negative evidence	a positive spin
30% of people disagree	70% of people agree

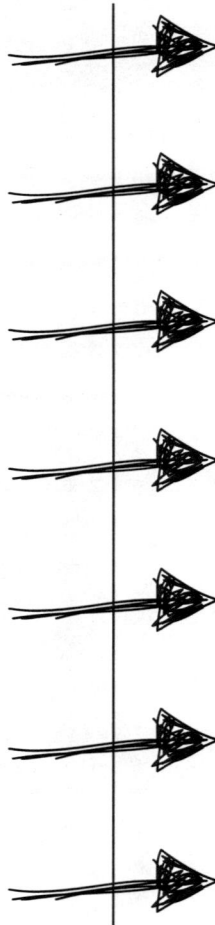

POSITIVITY IS IN THE EYE OF THE BEHOLDER

MOVE BEYOND WHAT WOULD **CONVINCE YOU**
TO IMAGINE WHAT WOULD **CONVINCE THEM**

arguments I would value   others might care about

it will fight global warming ——————▶   it will lower your gas pricess

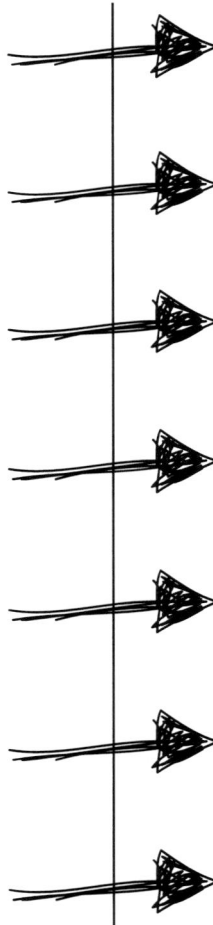

——————▶

——————▶

——————▶

——————▶

——————▶

——————▶

WHAT IF THEY SAY

SOMETHING THAT *offends?*

How can I disagree without shutting down dialogue?

I know you didn't mean it like that, but it sounded like...

**Think of three ways to acknowledge a bad impact
while assuming good intentions**

WHAT IF

SOMETHING YOU SAY OFFENDS?

IF ⊙→

A WORD
OFFENDS

I COULD SAY:

Wow, I did not know the history of that term, I'm so sorry...

IF ⊙→

A SOURCE
OFFENDS

I COULD SAY:

Wait, so you're saying that website is...

⊙→

⊙→

HOW CAN YOU HELP HEAL THE HURT, EVEN IF YOU DIDN'T MEAN TO OFFEND?

if you concede a little bit

it can make your argument more convincing

I know there have been some problems with this approach in the past, like...

think of some phrases to introduce a concession

DON'T MAKE THEM GUESS YOUR POINT. SAY IT ONE MORE TIME AT THE END!

in conclusion

So basically I think....

WHAT ARE SOME GOOD PHRASES TO MAKE PEOPLE PAY ATTENTION WHILE YOU SUM UP?

You did it! You finished!

HOW WILL YOU REWARD YOURSELF?

brainstorm here

THINGS I LEARNED FROM THIS WORKBOOK

☐ _____

☐ _____

☐ _____

☐ _____

☐ _____

☐ _____

☐ _____

☐ _____

☐ _____

☐ _____

☐ _____

☐ _____

☐ _____

☑ New   → A good reminder   ◻ Thinking about it   ☒ Struggling with it

I WILL TRY TO USE THESE TECHNIQUES

- [ ] _____
- [ ] _____
- [ ] _____
- [ ] _____
- [ ] _____
- [ ] _____
- [ ] _____
- [ ] _____
- [ ] _____

PRACTICE MAKES PERFECT

EVALUATE YOUR FIRST CHALLENGING CONVERSATION HERE

MY FIRST IMPRESSIONS OF THE CONVERSATION

_____
_____
_____
_____
_____

WHAT WENT WELL

_____
_____
_____
_____
_____

WHAT I WILL DO DIFFERENTLY NEXT TIME

_____
_____
_____
_____

PRACTICE MAKES PERFECT

EVALUATE YOUR SECOND CHALLENGING CONVERSATION HERE

MY FIRST IMPRESSIONS OF THE CONVERSATION

_____
_____
_____
_____
_____

WHAT WENT WELL

_____
_____
_____
_____
_____

WHAT I WILL DO DIFFERENTLY NEXT TIME

_____
_____
_____
_____
_____

PRACTICE MAKES PERFECT

EVALUATE YOUR THIRD CHALLENGING CONVERSATION HERE

MY FIRST IMPRESSIONS OF THE CONVERSATION

_____
_____
_____
_____
_____

WHAT WENT WELL

_____
_____
_____
_____
_____

WHAT I WILL DO DIFFERENTLY NEXT TIME

_____
_____
_____
_____
_____

Made in United States
Cleveland, OH
16 August 2025